BLUFF YOUR WAY IN MANAGEMENT

Joseph T. Straub
John Courtis

CENTENNIAL PRESS

ISBN 0-8220-2211-7

Centennial Press, Box 82087, Lincoln, Nebraska 68501
an imprint of Cliffs Notes, Inc.

INTRODUCTION

"Management" is an umbrella that covers a host of activities: leadership, working through others, planning, organizing, communicating, controlling, and making decisions, to name a few. How can you grasp all of these things? Fortunately, you don't have to.

The essence of bluffing your way in any activity is to keep control of a situation without enough information, assets, or power to justify that control. That, as it happens, is also the essence of management.

In some ways management needs no introduction. Most of us do it one way or another every day—in families, social groups, clubs, and businesses. Management is universal; it exists whenever two or more people try to do something together. You may not notice this, however, because only *mis*management makes headlines. Planes arrive late, companies go bankrupt, orders are lost, and the Pentagon pays defense contractors several hundred dollars for parts that cost a few bucks at Radio Shack because management has somehow failed.

People become managers by several routes. Those who work for family-owned firms inherit the job. Others may have worked their way up the organization or married the boss's son or daughter. Be especially suspicious of people who declare that they're "born managers," however. They can be identified by their total ignorance of management and their supreme confidence that their every decision is right.

But how can a bluffer masquerade as a real manager? Very easily, as it often turns out. Few managers really take the time to clarify or analyze their objectives, actions, and motives for what they do. If you, on the other hand, spend even a fragment of your work day thinking about what you're actually doing, you can rise above the rest of the pack. Especially if you maintain steady eye contact, dress neatly, and act sincere. In the words of George Burns, "Sincerity is everything. If you can fake that, you've got it made."

MANAGEMENT ACTIVITIES

Managers perform many activities. It's important for you to understand what each one involves so you can set goals, assign tasks, and delegate the authority to get them done right.

The major areas of a business include purchasing, production, sales, and finance. Service and retail businesses, which make no tangible product, still have a core of similar areas (minus production) that are vital to success. In fact, lots of people—especially those who sell insurance—now call services "products" to make them sound less vague and intangible. Bluffers have to understand the role of several key management activities that will help them deal with the major areas of a business successfully.

Decision Making

One of the problems with being a manager is that you have to make decisions from time to time. This can be very troublesome, because decisions can blow up in your face. But do you really *have* to decide? Sometimes not. If you want to sidestep a decision without looking indecisive, you can often fall back on philosophical quotations such as "Sometimes the best decision is no decision" and "If it works, don't fix it."

In any event, don't be intimidated into making a decision until you've analyzed the problem thoroughly.

Most panic decisions deal with *symptoms* of the problem and overlook the problem itself. If your car has a flat tire tomorrow morning, you could pump it up, but a block or two down the road it'll probably be flat again. You mistakenly treated the symptom (lack of air), when the actual problem (a hole) went unsolved.

Adroit bluffers also tend to let subordinates participate in making decisions. Go down to where the problem is and ask your workers, "What do you think is wrong?" Often, after they've recovered from the shock of being treated like people instead of robots, they'll tell you exactly what's wrong because they knew it all along. It's just that you're the first boss who ever bothered to ask. Follow up the previous question with "What do you think we should do about it?" This may produce several solutions that are worth their weight in gold. The end result is that you've shifted the burden of defining problems and solving them from yourself to everybody in your work group. And, if the decision backfires, it'll be more comforting to be able to stand up and say, "Well, *we* thought . . ." than to have to take all the blame yourself.

Delegating

Bluffers should be quick to delegate authority for routine decisions to subordinates. Delegation makes you look very professional. It also saves you time because you have to wrestle with only unusual, off-the-wall problems.

And how should you deal with those? Maybe the best thing to do is fall back on the suggestion offered a moment ago: call your subordinates together and have them propose what you should do. Emphasize, of course, that you're *not* relinquishing your authority. You're merely being a democratic leader who believes in lots of employee involvement. It won't hurt to point out that the Japanese make decisions by consensus and participation, and you're simply adopting a tried-and-true technique. It's tough for anybody to dispute the success of Japanese business these days.

Communicating

It's been argued that communication is one of the most valuable tricks of the management trade. Getting a simple message across the way you intended can be harder than it seems. People define words differently, have conflicting sets of priorities, and harbor hidden agendas that conspire to make communicating difficult.

One good rule of thumb is to follow the KISS technique – Keep It Simple, Stupid. Another guideline is to reject meaningless jargon. Because people write and speak to impress as well as to inform, they sometimes feel compelled to make memos and reports sound "businesslike" or profound. The result can be a pompous, indecipherable mess. If you believe you're the target of a verbal snow job from subordinates, assert yourself by sending back a memo or report to be rewritten. This puts people on notice that you're a no-nonsense, hard-headed manager who tells it like it is and expects others to do the same.

Accounting

Accounting is a fairly simple process. It's mostly a blend of basic math and common sense. The information, however, is often susceptible to manipulation and several interpretations. Bluffers should take the advice of U.S. Supreme Court Justice Robert H. Jackson, who said, "Success depends on knowing what not to believe in accounting."

The term "creative accounting" is a euphemism for doctoring the books to make a company look better than it is, while "conservative accounting" makes a company look mediocre or worse. Most corporations prefer to look like heroes to stockholders and bag ladies to the IRS.

Bluffers who encounter a mass of incomprehensible figures can cover their confusion with such phrases as: Do you really believe this bottom line is realistic? Have you checked for a recent FASB (Financial Accounting Standards Board) ruling on this? How much could this change between now and the end of the quarter? and Are you sure overhead has been allocated properly? Perhaps the best comment of all, however, is "You'll have to simplify this so the board of directors will understand it." That probably means that you'll be able to understand it too.

It's important to consider the impact of the notes at the end of accounting reports, because these can reveal situations or conditions that figures tend to hide. For example, one company discreetly admitted that it was so strapped for cash that it had borrowed on the cash surrender value of its president's life insurance policy. Another's report celebrated a rise in its stock price, but the cause was the death of its founder and president.

He was an autocratic octogenarian well past his prime, and investors apparently believed the business was better off without him. Notes may reveal what the figures conceal. Catchy slogan, isn't it?

Analyzing Cost Variances

This is what accountants do with the difference between budgeted costs and actual costs. Significant differences (which accountants insist on calling "variances") are reviewed and targeted for corrective action.

In many companies, accountants spend so much time identifying variances and making sure they're allocated to the right accounting period that they never get around to telling management what the variances mean or what might have caused them. Don't assume that accountants know the meaning or cause of every variance, and don't let them imply that you should, either. Make them give you a plain-language explanation of what caused the variances (you might insist on calling them "differences" to assert your position). If they don't know, make it clear that you expect them to find out and get back to you. Accountants may be bluffers too, so you have to be on your guard.

Exporting

"Export or die" is a highly overrated slogan. Bluffers should regard this as a choice between two legitimate alternatives, and the second one might not be too bad.

Exporting is a pain in the neck. If you're already doing it, it may be worth continuing, but you're always at the mercy of foreign exchange fluctuations, volatile political changes, legal problems, and bewildering cultural quirks that would challenge the patience of a diplomat or the President's chief of protocol. In at least one country, showing your host the sole of your shoe is a cultural insult serious enough to have you executed by a firing squad.

Even after you've budgeted for freight, insurance, uninsurable losses, tariffs, and selling expenses, there's still the cost of travel for managers who insist on checking out foreign facilities in person instead of making a phone call or looking at photographs. Some globe-trotting executives brag about having golf partners all over the world, and guess who pays the bill? Corporations often notice an abrupt increase in foreign travel just before major international sporting events.

Meetings

It's been said that managers have meetings only when they don't know what to do. That's not entirely true. They also have meetings when they know what to do, but want to share the responsibility, or when they want someone else to do it or suggest it.

Meetings of three or more people are inefficient and hazardous. Bluffers should avoid them. It's easier to disguise your ignorance or explain it casually one-on-one, but virtually impossible in front of a group. You may end up being exposed and handed your head.

Financing

Finance has close ties to accounting, and in fact, many people who work in finance may be accounting majors who couldn't pass the CPA exam. The folks in finance often work out ways to pay for things (such as recently acquired companies) by selling more stock (which they call "equity securities") or borrowing through the sale of bonds (which they call "debt securities"). The finance department may also field inquiries from stockholders and suggest how much profit, if any, will be paid to the stockholders as dividends each quarter.

Recruiting

Savvy recruiting is one of the most important weapons in the bluffer's arsenal because you need a team that you can delegate to without losing sleep or developing an ulcer. Most managers recruit so badly that you can look better than average by avoiding stupid mistakes.

A vacancy offers two choices. You can either fill the job or eliminate it. If you decide that the position is essential, proceed with care. Bluffers should hire candidates who meet two major criteria:

(1) They're competent enough to do their job but not ambitious enough to come after yours.

(2) They feel loyal to you for hiring them, so you can count on them to stand behind you in a crisis.

Some very bad managers have become successful largely through savvy recruiting.

Training

> I keep six honest serving men,
> They taught me all I knew;
> Their names are What and Why and When
> And How and Where and Who.

This passage from Rudyard Kipling's "The Elephant's Child" has lots of relevance in management. Use it as a guide when you are

- Preparing a presentation
- Explaining something in a training or orientation session
- Justifying a major project
- Writing a letter or memo

Testing what you write or say against these six key words helps you explain your point to others – and helps you understand it yourself.

Advertising

Don't fool around with advertising. Delegate the work to an outside ad agency. You can then plead ignorance (which is, of course, the truth) and crucify the agency if a campaign flops. Experts make ideal scapegoats when things go wrong.

Consider, for example, Burger King's Herb the Nerd campaign. It reportedly cost $40 million, but sales increased less than three percent. Customers saw Herb as an awful role model for anything – even a hamburger. McDonald's ads featuring John Houseman were zeros too because consumers didn't believe an aristocratic guy like Houseman would be caught dead in McDonald's. E. F. Hutton created an in-house campaign featuring Bill Cosby at a cost of some $6 million, but it bombed because Cosby's credibility with Jell-O and Ford cars didn't carry over to investments.

Managing Time

Bluffers know that management revolves around dealing with people and other resources. To do that well, you have to manage yourself. That boils down to managing your use of time. Good managers do this naturally or learn how to do it. Bad managers never master the art. Expert bluffers manage their time by

- Minimizing interruptions
- Setting aside thinking time
- Controlling meetings with an iron hand
- Refusing to get involved with activities that aren't connected with their objectives
- Demanding that subordinates never bring them problems without also proposing solutions
- Announcing to everyone within earshot that their schedule is packed, and they'd have trouble making time for one more meeting, conference, or obligation

A "my door is always open" philosophy can be one of the world's worst time-wasters. That policy, says former Continental Airlines president Robert F. Six, ". . . is guaranteed to turn on every whiner, lackey, and neurotic on the property."

You have to be available sometimes, of course, because you can't afford to isolate yourself from the mainstream of communications. The key is to make yourself accessible at *specific* times so your day isn't riddled by constant interruptions. Your secretary can serve as an excellent buffer (a bluffer's buffer, if you will) to defend your schedule against unwanted meetings, drop-in visitors, and casual employee chit-chat.

The two most common symptoms of poor time management are excessive overtime work and lugging work home at night and on weekends. If you're doing either, you should analyze how you spend your day. Some corporate cultures really value such self-abuse, however, and if yours is one, you may have no choice but to go with the flow – at least with overtime work. Taking work home is the easiest bluff of all, though. Who can tell if your briefcase is full or empty?

Manufacturing

Bluffers realize that all production doesn't have to be done in-house. In fact *most* of what you make might be subcontracted to outside vendors, and the end product could simply be put together at your plant. Many companies could sub out part or all of what they make and perhaps earn more money than they do by producing it in their own plant. When faced with a production problem, a bluffer should always ask, "Why can't this gadget be made cheaper, faster, or better outside?" and then assign someone to check it out.

Procurement

"Procurement" is a fancy word for "purchasing." A company's buyers (a.k.a. Procurement Agents or P.A.s) aren't noticed much until they screw something up, then all hell can break loose. A key part that's delivered late, shipped short, or not made to specs can shut down a whole production line. One automaker's plant ground to a halt for several hours when workers ran out of left-hand taillights. Delivery snafus are only half of the procurement problem, however. Overstocked items are the other half, but they can be dealt with by mysterious fires or burst water pipes followed by a claim to the insurance company.

It's not necessary to know anything about procurement except that P.A.s who don't complain or look harassed are probably

(1) Too lazy to round up new vendors who can make things cheaper, better, or faster than present ones,

(2) Taking kickbacks from the salespeople who sell to them,

or both.

PEOPLE IN MANAGEMENT

Accountants

Accountants are the second cousins of statisticians and librarians. They tend to be meticulous, orderly, cynical, short on humor, and long on precision. Not your typical fun folks. Bob Newhart used to joke about starring in a failed television series called "Frontier Accountant." Enough said?

Accountants, like other strange animals, come in several varieties. There's the Certified Public Accountant (CPA), the Certified Management Accountant (CMA), and in Great Britain the Chartered Accountant, which is very much like a CPA.

Accountants may suffer from persecution complexes and believe that they're unloved. They usually welcome friends from outside their function and can be good drinking buddies because they're often eager for companionship. Never try to outdrink an accountant, however, because most of them did brewery or distillery audits in their early days and have a high tolerance for alcohol.

Deal with accountants diplomatically. They can be nasty when cornered. If you attack their figures in a meeting, for example, they may let loose a barrage of financial jargon that leaves nonaccountants too shaken to answer coherently. Instead, go one-on-one with the accountants beforehand. Ask them to explain their figures, and listen respectfully and eagerly. Nod your head a lot. You'll find that this will get you a clear and patient outline of what their numbers really mean.

It pays to be nice to accountants because, aside from having lots of clout in today's bottom-line-oriented organizations, they also sign the paychecks.

Executives

"Executive" is a nebulous term that implies power, status, and the right to take a three-martini, two-hour lunch. The label is often reserved for higher-level managers, but its use varies from one company to the next. When you get right down to it, anybody who dresses neatly and totes a briefcase looks like an executive, so the title is pretty meaningless. Bluffers should feel free to adopt all the outward trappings of executive status. Nobody will object; most will be impressed.

Directors

The company's directors are supposed to manage the top managers. The directors, in turn, answer to the stockholders, who technically own the company.

Directors are paid well for being stockholder advocates and overseeing top management, but there's also a risk. Directors who rubber-stamp top management's requests without weighing all the facts and issues have been sued for malpractice by stockholders. Nevertheless, a corporate director has lots of status and plenty of perks, which makes the job worthwhile.

Some of the directors may themselves be accomplished bluffers. That's how they got to be directors.

Chairman of the Board

The chairman of the board is probably the most adroit bluffer in the boardroom. In addition, he or she has an above-average chance of getting publicly flayed if the company gets into trouble.

The chairman writes a letter to stockholders that usually appears on the first page of the company's annual report. It's not generally realized that this letter (which patronizingly refers to the business as "your company") isn't audited or critiqued. Consequently, it may contain several outrageous statements about the company's past, present, or future condition.

All bluffers need to remember is that the chairman has a vote when directors cast their ballots, so the time spent briefing or buddying up to the chairman can pay off if you want to get pet projects approved.

Marketing People

Marketing people are concerned with advertising, publicity, public relations, personal selling, customer service, distribution, and other things that are supposed to entice customers to buy and to keep 'em happy afterward.

Marketing, like politics, is an inexact science. Companies have trouble knowing which parts of marketing work and which ones don't. If you want to be quotable in a marketing crisis, you might repeat Sir Thomas Lipton's comment about advertising: "Half the money we spend on advertising is wasted, but we don't know which half." The idea applies to marketing in general.

Bluffers should memorize the buzz phrase "consumer orientation" because that's the point of view that most companies have (or *claim* they have) today. Every activity in the company is intended to satisfy consumer wants and needs, including those grueling top management strategy retreats in Hawaii, Bermuda, or the Virgin Islands. Good bluffers master the ability to defend these junkets with a straight face. In the immortal words of Malcolm Forbes, "There are more fakers in business than in jail."

Analysts

The title "Analyst" is confusing. To neurotic New Yorkers and Hollywood residents, it means psychiatrist. To a few people in the real (nonbusiness) world, it can mean chemist. In business, however, it's likely to refer to the sharper end of the accounting or finance department. This includes accountants who want to be something else and MBAs and others who are passing through the finance department on their way up the corporate ladder. In major multinational corporations people are often given the title of analyst when they're doing a good job but have run out of promotional opportunities. Analysts tend to be perceptive, ambitious, and perhaps a tad insecure.

Nowhere is this more true than with bright people who work for major brokerage firms. These people assume that they'll make it to the top because they're sharper than the partners. Unfortunately, there'll come a time when they realize that there's room for only one sharp partner at a time. Because the incumbent sharp partner probably drinks less than the rest, it may be some time before he or she dies, retires, or moves. Until then, analysts will have to be content with remaining where they are.

Bluffers can cash in on this condition. Financial analysts in major brokerage firms are incorruptible, cynical, clinical observers of the companies that they investigate and write reports about. If they're analyzing yours, and if you detour them into a sympathetic discussion of their problems and career path, they may file a more favorable report of your company's value as an investment. Such discreet ego stroking ultimately causes your company's stock price to rise. If you've participated in the employee stock ownership plan, you could reap a handsome personal payoff.

Sales Reps

The sales function, which is part of marketing, is critical to a company's survival. You can do without lots of other functions, but no sales mean no business.

Alas, sales reps are underrecognized, and because they are, it's hard to get bright, ambitious people to build a career in sales. And since there aren't too many bright, ambitious people in sales, they tend to be underrecognized. The cycle feeds on itself.

Fortunately, this isn't your problem unless you're in sales or your job directly depends on it. Stay aloof from semantic debates about sales being part of marketing or vice-versa. Above all, try not to get involved in hiring sales applicants. It can drive you crazy. They all claim they're above average until you press for factual evidence; then they suddenly become substandard, indeed. If many sales applicants worked as hard at selling their products as they do at trying to impress interviewers, they might not be unemployed so often.

If you *must* hire salespeople, hire the best listeners you can find. People can't sell customers what they want until they've listened to those customers. Good listeners will ultimately make good managers—and good bluffers. It also helps if the people you hire are tall, dress sharply, and have a firm handshake and a granite profile.

FACETS OF MANAGEMENT

Facets of management are a grab bag of activities that can't be allocated to one group of specialized managers.

The things that follow have an impact on the organization in general and on dedicated bluffers in particular. If profits are overemphasized, we make no apology. No profits mean no jobs for bluffers or anyone else, so profits are essential.

Statistics

All you need to know about statistics is that they're easily manipulated and likely to be wrong. Don't bother saying "There are lies, damned lies, and statistics" because everyone's heard it by now.

It's important to remember that *all* statistics are wrong in some respect. Samples, for instance, are often biased. If the sample and other aspects of a study are on the level, then the context in which they're communicated may be misleading. For example, a Russian and an American car had a race several years ago and the Russian car lost. *Pravda* reported that the Russian car came in second, but the American car was next to last. Then there's a masterpiece of deception used by would-be weight-watchers: "My weight's just fine. I'm six inches too short." For information on the more dazzling points of statistical footwork read *How to Lie with Statistics*, by Darrell Huff. It's a classic that belongs in every bluffer's library.

Profits

Profits, as mentioned earlier, are the Holy Grail of most companies. It isn't enough to know this as a broad principle. The way to earn profits and "attaboys" at the same time is to make it clear that you're dedicated to earning today's profit today, this week's this week, and so on, because you won't get a second chance. Don't worry about living up to this motto, because few management information systems are sophisticated enough to report profits by the day or week anyway. As far as bluffers are concerned, profit can be improved by doing one or a combination of three simple things: (1) cutting costs, (2) raising prices, and (3) increasing sales.

Loss

Loss is the opposite of profit. If you're explaining or planning to avoid a loss, remember that a loss can occur from selling things for less than they cost to make or buy (stupid and thoroughly avoidable) or from letting expenses grow out of control (somewhat avoidable) or from not selling enough to cover expenses. The latter condition often leads to an overhaul of your sales force and/or sales forecasting techniques. Some long faces and pink slips are a likely result.

Companies may report a profit to stockholders and

a loss to the IRS. Sound strange? Not to accountants. "Creative accounting," coupled with IRS regulations, allows companies to figure things one way on financial reports and a different way on tax returns. Equipment, for example, may be depreciated faster for tax accounting purposes than for financial accounting purposes. Inventories may be valued using several methods too, and that can make the difference between a profit and a loss. If this implies that companies keep two sets of books—one for financial accounting and another for tax accounting—you're right.

Cash Flow

Cash flow can be lots more important than profits. A company can have billions in assets and run out of cash to pay next week's bills. Collecting the money you've earned is vital to survival unless you have unlimited resources or can use someone else's money. The government does this all the time.

Anyway, positive cash flow means money is coming in faster than it's being paid out. This doesn't necessarily mean that the company is profitable, only that it can pay its bills when they're due. After all, positive cash flow can happen when a company sells off assets or borrows short-term money. Whatever the case, positive cash flow is usually a good thing because, as somebody (perhaps a bluffer) once said, "If your outgo exceeds your income, your upkeep will be your downfall." Collect what's owed you as soon as possible, but don't pay out a dime until you absolutely must.

Insurance

The concept of insurance has been around since Greek and Roman times. If your business is big enough, you may decide not to insure the full value of a particular asset, just like car owners sometimes elect a high deductible in exchange for lower premiums.

Deciding which risks to accept, which to insure, and how to remove or reduce exposure in general is called "risk management." Companies that accept risks instead of insuring against them sometimes set up a fund (called a "self-insurance fund") that will be used to replace certain assets if they're destroyed, and heaven help any employees who were responsible for the damage.

Budgets

Budgets are the tools that most managers use to control their areas of responsibility. They are tightly tied to variances, which we mentioned earlier.

Budgets deal with the future. They project the costs, expenses, and profits expected from certain "profit centers," which may be a product, a company subsidiary, or some other business unit.

Bluffers who take over a job midway into the budget period must proceed with care. Things are even more incomprehensible than they were when the budget was first set up. Acceptable phrases to use while trying to get your bearings are

- Did my predecessor actually *approve* this budget?
- What allocations are in here that we don't control?

- Are we going to change the budget based on recent market changes?
- I don't think we're aware of all the costs allocated against this area. Who's authorizing them?

Even in the best-managed companies, one or more of these questions are bound to buy you time.

Zero-Based Budgeting

American political scientist Aaron Wildavsky once observed, "The largest determining factor of the size and content of this year's budget is last year's budget." The concept of ZBB tries to avoid repeating historical mistakes by developing next year's budget *without* referring to last year's. Every year stands on its own; every item must be justified anew.

Human nature being what it is, a new budget will rarely be developed without someone sneaking a peek at the old one and screaming about the discrepancies. This is inevitable and beneficial. The discrepancies will prove one of three things:

(1) The managers who developed that budget didn't understand last year's revenues or expenses, for reasons that should now be explored.
(2) Historical figures were incorrectly analyzed or allocated.
(3) The company could operate fine under the new zero-based figures if management tries hard enough.

Return on Investment

This yardstick is useful for measuring the performance of a business or a profit center, but it isn't much fun when it's used against you.

The problem is that the fixed assets that seem so necessary when you view them individually can suddenly ruin your relative performance. Fixed assets are like fat. The more you can get rid of without damaging your (financial) health, the better off you are. Uncollected debts, raw materials, work in process, finished goods, and goods in transit all conspire to depress your ROI. This is a good incentive to reduce all of them.

Bluffers should also know that companies may avoid buying new and better equipment just to maintain an impressive ROI. If the old equipment is already fully depreciated, no depreciation is charged against this year's profits. Unfortunately, managers who play this game postpone the inevitable. They're mortgaging the future for the present.

Minimizing Taxes

There are two ways to minimize taxes. One is evasion, which is illegal and may land you in a minimum-security country club at government expense for a year or two. The other way is through avoidance. This is legal; go for it. In practice, what usually happens is that someone cooks up a scheme and discovers it's illegal; then the company spends lots of money on expensive lawyers and accountants who ultimately make it legal by lobbying to change the tax code or to get a favorable ruling from the IRS.

If you can't afford to go this route, then minimize your tax liability by flogging your accountants so they earn every cent of their salary. Explore every angle; leave no stone or chapter of the tax code unturned. Also defer paying whatever taxes you do owe as long as possible.

It's quite acceptable to ask, "What's the *real* after-tax effect?" because too many corporate presentations make no mention of tax or treat it as a foregone conclusion. Most corporate decisions have tax implications. It's better to be the one who draws attention to a potential pitfall than to have to describe in detail why a newly hatched scheme won't work. You get credit for identifying the problem. The poor wretch who has to research the tax consequences and tell higher management how the IRS will gouge the company for taxes eventually takes the heat. Better him than you, though. When there's bad news, top bosses sometimes shoot the messenger.

Mergers

See Acquisitions. There's no such thing as a merger.

Value Analysis

Value analysis means what it says. You analyze the value of the parts that go into a product to figure out if you can make them from cheaper or less-durable material. Components that outlast the rest of the product are good candidates for value analysis. Ideally, the end product should collapse in a heap when it has exhausted its useful life.

Value analysis can also be applied to the services your organization uses as well as the reports and staff functions that may have been created without much forethought over the years. Bluffers should challenge such things as the frequency and number of reports issued by various departments, the number of people on the distribution lists, and the amount and type of data that are recorded and reported by their own department. If the cost of something exceeds its benefit, it's a prime target for elimination.

Management Succession

Management succession isn't a synonym for management development. Lots of companies believe in developing managers but give little or no thought to management succession. This is because they either assume you need several decades of experience before you qualify to be promoted one rung or because the chief executive believes he's immortal and has no intention of retiring. Symptoms of the latter condition include a parade of potential successors who come in as assistant to the patriarch and eventually leave out of frustration. Bluffers shouldn't join this parade because it usually leads to nowhere.

Earnings Per Share

Earnings per share can be more important than profits or cash flow as far as stockholders are concerned. Earnings per share are the true measure of a company's growth and management's effectiveness (or lack of it). Be careful about announcing that you've improved your company's earnings per share, however. This has the embarrassing side effect of reminding people (particularly analysts and journalists) to compare your corporate performance with competitors', and the contrast may not be flattering.

Management Buyout

A management buyout is a peculiar deal in which top managers, with or without the help of external financing, buy all or part of a business from the present stockholders.

Management buyouts are usually done for the wrong reasons. If the company is profitable, the top managers shouldn't be able to afford to buy it. If it's losing money, they should have more sense than to buy it. The situation is like a poker game in that both sides have different views of the business and its future. One or both sides must be bluffing, otherwise it would be impossible to agree on a price. After the buyout, managers will probably work harder, better, or smarter than they did when they were employees. This tells you something about how hard they worked before the buyout.

Acquisitions

Corporate acquisitions are sexy and macho—the ultimate power trip. You're playing Monopoly with real companies. If you're secure in your job, it's possible to be more dispassionate about them. When an acquisition looms up, few people have the guts to ask any of the following questions:

- Couldn't we start from scratch cheaper and better?
- Will the customers stay if we buy it?
- Why do the current owners want to sell?
- Why not let the target company go bankrupt and buy the assets at a bargain price?
- What else could we do with the money?

The last question is best kept in reserve, but any one of these can make you look thoughtful and competent when everyone else has caught acquisition fever. Fact: audits of most acquisitions show that they failed to earn the profits or other benefits that the acquiring firm expected. It's therefore good management practice to play the devil's advocate when talking about acquisitions. In the words of Robert Frost, "Take care to sell your horse before he dies. The art of living is passing losses on."

Management Audit

"Management audit" is a euphemism designed to convince young accountants that they're doing more than a traditional internal audit. Ignore it.

Most of the time accountants are innocuous and won't stray far from auditing numbers. When they do, their grasp of the business is usually so weak that any findings can be rebutted without referring to the facts. You can then fix the problems they've uncovered after they leave.

Management Development

The term "management development" implies a program that will move promising managers through a series of positions to broaden their experience and qualify them for major responsibilities. The chosen few may boast that they're on the "fast track" to the top, which often means they'll develop ulcers and hypertension five years earlier than the rest of us.

Some developmental moves are actually intended to detour certain candidates from the "fast track" without their knowing it until it's too late.

Bluffers may have to work closely with the victims of management development programs who rotate through various departments. Not to worry. Most fast-trackers are so confused by the amount of information they're expected to assimilate that they can barely function, let alone catch on to the fact that you're a bluffer.

Employees

Lots of organizations have begun calling employees "human resources" or "associates." No matter what the buzz word, they're still just people. Honest.

The more employees you have, the more headaches you're likely to get. Employees can find an almost endless list of things to sue you for, including age, sex, and racial discrimination, sexual harassment, unlawful discharge, and (if you badmouth one to a prospective employer) defamation of character.

Savvy bluffers should investigate a fairly new concept that can make people problems disappear like magic: employee leasing. First, you fire your entire work force (sound good so far?) and an employee leasing company hires them. Then you rent them back from the leasing company. Now, if you discover you've got a troublemaker, you just call the leasing company and ask it to send you somebody else. With any luck, they'll place the soreheads, militants, malcontents, and goof-offs with one of your competitors. The leasing company keeps the records, writes the paychecks, and administers other exciting details that your company used to do to maintain a work force. You, on the other hand, are free to do what you always intended to do — run a business for profit.

Hobbies

Managers don't have hobbies. Grim, serious recreational pursuits maybe, but never hobbies. Bluffers need to become good at racquetball or tennis, which are fine outlets for the frustration encountered on the job. These activities also portray you as an aggressive competitor, which is what companies expect every manager to be.

It should go without saying that you must know how to play golf. It's the universal management sport. If you don't play, you'll isolate yourself from coworkers who probably hatch more schemes on the golf course than they do at the office.

Status Symbols

Status symbols can be formal or informal, but they all bespeak clout — or lack of it.

Formal status symbols tend to come with promotion. In other words, you have to earn them. They're badges of rank in the corporate army. Some of the most common ones are

- Reserved parking space next to the building
- Office with a window (corner offices and those on top floors best)
- Executive dining room privileges
- Wet bar in office
- Jacuzzi adjoining office
- Cellular car phone supplied by the company
- Private secretary
- First-class travel privileges
- Designer lamps and furniture

Although bluffers might not qualify for some of the above status symbols, they may be able to come up with reasonable facsimiles. Perhaps you don't rate a reserved parking spot right next to the building, for example, but maybe you can wangle one in the reserved *lot*, which is better than hiking three blocks from the general parking area like the rest of the peons. Make it your business to say nice things to the secretary who handles such matters. It also pays to befriend people like the head of facilities and maintenance, who would be in a position to install a better office rug or wallpaper than you deserve. Check Dale Carnegie's timeless book *How to Win Friends and Influence People* for the finer points of dealing with such folks.

You may decide it's politically expedient to spend your own money for things that the company won't supply, such as a cellular phone and high-class office furnishings. Outsiders, new employees, and casual visitors who don't know the difference will think your expensive trappings came with the territory. If somebody is rude enough to ask, "How did you rate this?" just smile and shrug your shoulders. That adds to your mystique.

Informal status symbols are another matter. These are often adopted by the informal organization, and their importance varies from one company or department to the next. For example, *Personal Computing* reported that some managers like to display popular computer software as status symbols, although they may not even know how to run it. The more impressive programs are *Lotus 1-2-3, Symphony, dBase III, Harvard Project Manager,* and the latest release of MS-DOS or PC-DOS. It's noteworthy that there are some computer games on the market that, with the touch of a key, will throw a model of a spreadsheet up on your monitor. A handy feature for when your boss walks in the door.

Most informal status symbols revolve around personal or office accessories. These include Rolex watches, Mont Blanc pens, designer leather portfolios and briefcases, and personal computer systems with lots of bells and whistles. As a Bluffer, you should consider acquiring one or more of these because ultimately they may prove to be an investment in your career. A PC system at home that's linked by modem to your office machine, for example, implies that you're a dedicated manager who may need to summon the electronic genie at any hour of the night and download or upload data from your office files. It doesn't hurt to be seen carrying a portable PC to and from work, either. You certainly look more progressive and farsighted than colleagues who are carrying briefcases. The intimidation value alone can be priceless.

Bankruptcy

Bankruptcy happens when a company's debts exceed its assets. Businesses that are about to go under usually file for protection under Chapter 11 of the bankruptcy code. This holds the creditors at bay while management tries to reorganize the company and come up with a plan to pay them off. Creditors may go along with this because they realize it's better to collect the entire debt late than to get fifty cents on the dollar on time. If the company can't come up with an acceptable payoff schedule, however, its assets are liquidated and the business goes down the tubes. That's what happened to the W. T. Grant department store chain.

Bluffers should keep an eye out for symptoms of impending bankruptcy. These include

- Top managers driving Mercedes or BMWs with vanity license tags
- A new fountain in the reception area at corporate headquarters
- The chairman of the board being honored for his service to various charitable organizations — but not to the company
- A salesperson or engineer being promoted to chief executive officer
- A recent move to new corporate headquarters
- An unqualified or elderly chief financial officer
- A chairman who used to be a politician, actor, or astronaut

- Satisfied employees who have not threatened to go on strike for several years
- A fast-track management development candidate who is promoted to chief operating officer

We are indebted to Bill Mackey, a senior partner of Ernst & Whinney, for the above list, which he claims is a more reliable guide to bankruptcy than ratio analysis. We believe it. And we would add two more items:

- A chairman who becomes president of a trade association
- The company's history being published in hardback

MANAGEMENT STYLES

Management styles are generally a lot of baloney. If you know the difference between Douglas McGregor's Theory X (negative attitude) and Theory Y (positive attitude) managers, you know enough. All the theories merely *describe* management styles. They won't help you change yours a bit. Managers adopt a style unconsciously, and once adopted, it becomes very difficult to change. Studies by *Fortune* and other business magazines have revealed that successful companies are run by chief executives with styles that range from participative to downright vicious, and all the companies make money. Even managers who try to change their styles often revert to their old habits in a crisis.

For bluffers, the key to management style is *be consistent*. As long as your people know what to expect from you, things will work out all right. As one executive put it, "I know I'm an SOB, but I'm a consistent one, so nobody gets surprised."

Leadership

"Leadership" is an issue only when it's absent. People who think about it a lot aren't leaders. Natural leaders don't bother to think about how to lead, and they've never considered any other role. Don't discuss leadership. Trying to define a good leader, or even list the qualities of one, is like nailing Jell-O to a tree.

Genius

Genius is all right in its place. You can tolerate geniuses at work as long as they don't tell you they belong to Mensa. If they do, fire them immediately. Your preferred position is to have been a member of Mensa but to have resigned when you found that the others joined mostly to bolster their insecurities about dealing with the real world. Being a genius doesn't make you a good manager, although being a good bluffer may earn you the reputation of a genius. Perhaps An Wang said it best: "Success is more a function of common sense than it is of genius."

Innovation

If you're running like mad to stay in the same place, the added strain of having to produce innovative products, services, or internal systems and practices won't be welcome.

We have nothing against innovation. Somebody has to do it. The trouble is, innovations won't sell themselves. It's a myth that the world will beat a path to your door if you invent a better mousetrap. You'll also have to manufacture, package, finance, and market it. Things can get complicated in a hurry.

Tactically, bluffers should endorse innovative thinking but delegate the task of implementing the ideas to somebody else. Creative thinking can be lots of fun, but the party's over when you find yourself stuck with implementing the blockbuster idea you've dreamed up. An organization needs both dreamers and doers, and it's best to delegate the nuts and bolts of applying an innovation to a doer. Or else have lots of reasons for shelving the idea until later.

Management by Exception

A close cousin to delegation, management by exception is the maxim that you should get involved only with unusual problems or work that can't be delegated. Managing by exception saves you lots of time, because you don't spend useless hours examining or working with situations that don't require your attention. Never mind the things that are going along fine. Invest your energy in dealing with problem areas. That makes perfect sense.

Assertiveness

Assertiveness is worth further study if you want to be professional about your impact on people. In their book *Assertiveness at Work*, Ken and Kate Back describe assertiveness as follows:

- Standing up for your own rights in such a way that you don't violate someone else's rights
- Expressing your needs, wants, opinions, feelings, and beliefs directly, honestly, and appropriately

All managers need to master the art of assertiveness. Being too nice, giving in when you know you're right, or failing to state your case will undermine your effectiveness with peers, subordinates, and superiors alike.

Bluffers should realize that both aggressive and non-assertive people can be conquered by the persistent application of assertiveness. Assertiveness might be described as sugar-coated aggression (you're not belligerent or obnoxious), and adept bluffers practice assertiveness with all the determination of a pit bull after a mail carrier.

The Managerial Grid

The Managerial Grid is a handy way to summarize someone's management style. The grid relates the degree to which managers feel concerned for production as compared to people. For example, a 1,9 manager has a low regard for production and a high regard for people—a "country clubber" who may worry more about being liked than getting the work out. A 9,1 manager, on the other hand, is obsessed with productivity and treats people like interchangeable parts. Managers who come in at 5,5 on the grid have balanced but not maximized their concern for both areas. The ideal position on the grid is 9,9 because this means you have both balanced and maximized concern for production and people. Don't expect to meet many of these folks.

You don't need to remember which scale is which. Most people have forgotten anyway.

Motivation

There are lots of management theories about motivation, but relatively little attention is paid to it in practice. It's good to be able to reel off the names of the heaviest hitters in the field, who are Douglas McGregor, Frederick Herzberg, and Abraham Maslow. Bluffers should also realize that motivational theories don't work on employees who detest their jobs. Qualifications notwithstanding, bluffers should hire applicants who really seem to *like* the kind of work the company offers because if they don't, you won't be able to motivate them worth a hoot.

If you want to motivate people, the ground rules are fairly simple:

(1) Pay them fairly and give them a chance to earn more by performing above average.
(2) Let them know why their jobs exist and how their work relates to the company's objectives.
(3) Treat them like mature human beings who want to work and will support the company's objectives, once they know what those objectives are.
(4) Praise exceptional effort and achievement and give prompt, tactful guidance if performance falls below standards.
(5) Encourage questions, no matter how basic.

Motivation is like leadership and sex. Those who do it best practice it and enjoy it but they don't tend to talk a lot about it.

Role-Playing

Bluffers pretending to be managers are no news to us. Adults acting like children are commonplace in business too. What is less acceptable are various other roles that people adopt, consciously or unconsciously, during the working day. Role-playing is an essential tool in training activities, but the ability to spot it and/or use it tactically on the job is even more important. Knowing that it exists is more than half the battle.

Bluffers need to develop the ability to spot people who seem to be playing a role versus those who are being themselves. Role-players lack conviction and commitment, which often means they can be manipulated or intimidated more easily than others.

Performance Appraisal

Performance appraisal is becoming more popular. Avoid it like the plague because you'll open a can of worms no matter what you say. Good people know they're good, and they usually don't want to hear about their inconsequential weaknesses. Nitpicking just makes them mad. Average people will sink into a depression if you remind them that they're as far from the bottom as from the top. This won't help their performance, and you'll end up feeling guilty. Below-average people can be devastated by being told about faults that they have neither the brains nor the personality to surmount.

Bluffers should transfer below-average people to somebody else's department and choose their replacements carefully. In fact, below-average performers may not have to be replaced at all, because they weren't doing much anyway. If you allocate their work to the average and good people in your group, business will continue as usual.

Management by Objectives (MBO)

MBO works well when it's done properly. It begins with the manager and the employee jointly setting the goals the employee will try to reach during the next work period. The goals are expressed quantitatively, so there's no debate about whether they were accomplished and you have a yardstick to measure and help the employee if necessary.

The two of you should meet periodically to see if the goals should be changed in light of unforeseen circumstances, and at the end of the period, you'll jointly evaluate how well the worker did.

Even if there's no company-wide MBO program, you should do this within your own department. You'll understand your subordinates' work and help them understand their responsibilities and the wider goals involved.

If you're the victim of a bad MBO program, you can use the things that make it bad to discredit it. These things will almost certainly include

- Failing to agree on objectives that subordinates will reach
- Setting objectives late in the work period
- Setting unrealistic objectives
- Failing to monitor employees' performance or discuss deviations with them
- Failing to revise objectives when changes take place in the original conditions or circumstances under which they were set
- Failing to set objective (quantified) goals

MANAGEMENT—
GOOD AND BAD

The secret of good management is to avoid bad management. Likewise, the test of good managers is that they aren't remembered for the mistakes or idiosyncrasies that make bad managers so hard to forget. In other words, good managers are sometimes camouflaged by their own competence—and that's not always bad.

By adopting a low profile, bluffers are in an excellent position to display this symptom of good management. Good managers won't

- Panic
- Abuse subordinates
- Blame people
- Lose their temper
- Jump to conclusions
- Be afraid of change
- Confuse action with thought
- Fall in love with a product or project
- Stop learning
- Talk more than they listen
- Use "necessity" as an excuse for anything
- Worry

Good management is not necessarily characterized by charisma or excellence. It's often just a matter of being right more than 90 percent of the time and avoiding the gross mistakes of peers and predecessors. This knowledge should be especially comforting to bluffers. Note, however, that good management does *not* mean avoiding risk. Calculated risk is crucial to business growth. Stupid mistakes are not.

Seven Deadly Sins

The fact that we lump the following items under "deadly" sins doesn't imply that there are only seven management sins. There are probably about seventy significant ones. Nevertheless, here are seven of the things that managers should not do. Read on.

Worry

Don't do it. If something goes wrong, you're either able to fix the situation or you aren't. If you're able to take action, think about it first, then explore your options, evaluate the consequences, and move forward. If your hands are tied, concentrate on something that you *can* influence, and in the meantime the problem that was beyond your control may shrink to more manageable proportions. Mountains, in time, may become molehills so that when they surface again they or the circumstances surrounding them may have changed, or your subconscious may have produced a solution you didn't think of before. Worry, per se, has no place in management.

MSU

The Malady of Spurious Urgency afflicts most managers from time to time. In moments of crisis or when you're under pressure, you'll be tempted to allocate unreasonably high priorities to matters that in real terms are either trivial or not as important as they seem. The Malady of Spurious Urgency is closely related to the compulsion to do something – anything – in a crisis. The acid test of a manager who works well under pressure is that he or she is the only one *not* immediately doing something. The real manager thinks before acting. Even if it's only a bluff.

Weasel Words

Lots of people play political games in the typical organization. This usually means that they're too weak or devious to get results by normal methods. One interesting symptom is that, although they don't produce outright lies, they crank out more than their share of "weasel words" in internal documents.

Weasel words make messages impersonal, remote, and sterile. The literary eunuchs who use them are often afraid to accept personal responsibility for the opinion or position, so they use language as a shield. Consider the following examples and what they really mean:

A survey is being made of this.	I need more time to think of an answer.
Administrative oversight	I screwed up.
Growing body of opinion	Two managers agree.
Opinion widely held	Three managers agree.
Present indications are	One wild guess is as good as another.

This office is concerned.	Knock it off; I've got your number.
I made a strategic misrepresentation.	I lied.
This office cannot approve.	I won't let you.
In the amount of	For
According to our records	I found
On the occasion of	When
In the event of	If
We are in receipt of	I got
Kindly advise the under-signed.	Please let me know.
Pursuant to our agreement	As we agreed
I am not in a position to	I can't/won't
At that point in time	Then
At this point in time	Now

Bluffers should refuse to let subordinates use oatmeal-flavored language to deflect responsibility or avoid standing behind an issue. There are times, however, when a bluffer may want to do that very thing, and that's why we gave you this list. Use it in good health.

Spelling and Grammatical Errors in Correspondence

Those who don't like you will cite your errors as proof that you're an illiterate ignoramus. Those who are on your side will be disappointed in you.

People always assume that the errors are your fault, not your secretary's. After all, you're responsible for the condition of the correspondence that goes out above your signature. If your secretary is a master proofreader who covers your literary backside, you may still have a problem. She'll privately hold you in contempt and may relay this attitude to others in your organization via the grapevine. ("He makes ten times as much as I do, but he couldn't spell *cat* if you spotted him the *c* and the *a*.")

There's no excuse for this weakness, but there are two possible defenses. If you're reviewing a faulty document in front of colleagues, you may say brightly

(1) I think we have the early, uncorrected copy. I don't always spot wrong spelling since I took that Evelyn Wood speed reading course.
(2) I ground this out last night at home on my word processor, and I'm lousy on a keyboard. When we're finished talking about it, I'll rework it into a final draft.

Thinking the Worst

Relatively few people really try to do something damaging or destructive. If they're on your own team, the chances are even slimmer. It follows that when you're trying to understand the actions of someone else in the organization, there's usually a good reason for them. If the action or the results are negative, there are two possible reasons. The first is that the corporate context hasn't been explained to the person. This is a classic problem, and it happens when managers delegate tasks instead of objectives. The second reason is failure to follow up on something that started out right but went wrong somewhere along the way.

Good managers who are faced with apparent disasters assume the best but analyze the situation impartially to find out what went wrong and prevent a recurrence. (Bluffers please take note.) Bad managers, by contrast, assume the worst, suspect sabotage, point fingers of blame, and generally reveal their paranoia and personality defects to everyone involved.

Being Late

This sin is perpetuated by bosses, colleagues, and subordinates alike. It's totally unacceptable, because it implies irresponsibility, disorganization, and a cavalier attitude toward the organization's welfare and the business at hand. It's also contagious.

Relying on Second-Hand Communications

Good managers value the ability to communicate effectively. If you really want to score maximum points in this area, you have to be an alert receiver as well as a sender.

Mistrust all second-hand communications. Other things being equal, you can be certain that people, no matter what their intentions, will distort the messages they relay. Consider, for instance, the following example (source unknown) that makes the point extremely well:

OPERATION HALLEY'S COMET

A colonel issued the following directive to his executive officer:

"Tomorrow evening at approximately 20:00 hours Halley's Comet will be visible in this area, an event which occurs only once every 75 years. Have the men fall out in the battalion area in fatigues, and I will

50

explain this rare phenomenon to them. In case of rain, we will not be able to see anything, so assemble the men in the theater and I will show them films of it."

Executive officer to company commander: "By order of the colonel, tomorrow at 20:00 hours, Halley's Comet will appear above the battalion area. If it rains, fall the men out in fatigues, then march to the theater, where the rare phenomenon will take place, something which occurs once every 75 years."

Company commander to lieutenant: "By order of the colonel in fatigues at 20:00 hours tomorrow evening, the phenomenal Halley's Comet will appear in the theater. In case of rain in the battalion area, the colonel will give another order, something that occurs once every 75 years."

Lieutenant to sergeant: "Tomorrow at 20:00 hours, the colonel will appear in the theater with Halley's Comet, something which happens once every 75 years. If it rains, the colonel will order the comet into the battalion area."

Sergeant to squad: "When it rains tomorrow at 20:00 hours the phenomenal 75-year-old General Halley, accompanied by the colonel, will drive his Comet through the battalion theater in his fatigues."

The classic case of distortion in business is one where all good intentions run in the same direction and compound the problem. Assume, for example, that you want a gift of gourmet pears to arrive on or just before a friend's birthday, and you know the person will return home, at the latest, the day before. If you have your secretary order delivery on the 30th, knowing that the 31st is the birthday, a secretary with initiative will probably add a one-day safety margin to allow for the uncertainty of the Postal Service (a.k.a. the U.S. Snail). The grower, also no stranger to the Postal Service, will add yet another day to the secretary's—and we now have delivery scheduled for the 28th. Just to be safe, the shipping department may ship the order early enough to arrive on the 27th. The result is that your friend finds a three-day-old box of rotten pears on the doorstep when he comes home on the 30th.

Other indirect communication failures are less simple, but the principle remains the same—communicate or verify directly, one-on-one. Second-hand communication, like a second-hand car, may have been disassembled and put back together wrong.

THE OUTSIDE WORLD

There's a tendency for organizations of every size to ignore the things that happen in the real (nonbusiness) world. In its extreme form, this can lead to terminal megalomania, but even mild cases can cause shock and confusion when reality rears its ugly head.

It's not necessary to describe all the outside forces of evil here. The sample that follows includes those most likely to rattle your cage and intrude on your personal space.

Unions

History confirms that managers brought unions on themselves. Unions exist only because managers failed to give employees decent pay, benefits, and working conditions. Workers know when they're getting the short end of the stick, and unions, since the 1930s, have helped them break that stick off and beat management over the head with it.

Bluffers should treat their people well, whether unionized or not. If employees are unionized, good voluntary treatment makes the union appear unnecessary and ineffective – and, in fact, workers may come to agree and vote the union out. If employees aren't unionized, good treatment ensures that they'll be content to stay that way.

Actuaries

Actuaries wanted to be accountants, but they couldn't stand the excitement. They're usually brilliant mathematicians and statisticians, so don't cross them on their own numerical turf.

It's unlikely that you'll meet many actuaries, because most of them toil in solitude in the catacombs of insurance companies, where management slides their lunch under the door once a day and garnishes it with a paycheck once a month.

Actuaries have little contact with the world of industry, perhaps even with reality, but if you're working in insurance you may cross their path. Be kind to them. They're responsible for your auto insurance premiums.

Bankers

Treat bankers with caution. If you're lucky, you won't have much to do with them at all. There are only two rules when dealing with bankers.

The first rule is, when things are going well and bankers notice enough to say so, ask them for money. More money than you need.

The second rule is, don't ignore them when things are going badly. Tell them how bad things are and when conditions might get better. If possible, deliver the improvements earlier or better than you predicted. This helps bankers look good to examiners from the FDIC and the Fed.

Bankers are really very simple organisms and quite

Pavolvian in their reactions. If you have a choice, try to find an optimistic banker. He'll eventually be fired or demoted, but in the meantime he'll be an easy source of short-term money.

Government

Business is ambivalent about government. On one hand, the present administration represents the elected power in the country and the supreme democratic authority. On the other hand, there's a creeping suspicion that voters are a bunch of subnormal wimps, many of them not bright enough to work for a top-notch company, and others too dependent on government assistance programs to become self-supporting members of society.

This perception naturally leads to grave reservations about the ability and competency of the people those voters elected. Many legislators are believed not to understand business and to lack the personal qualities necessary to rise high in any organization except government. Once elected, however, a legislator's ability to fool some of the people all of the time can be enough to provide job security, flexible working hours, deep-discount lunches, chauffeured limousines, "fact-finding" trips to exotic foreign countries, and an opulent office with a view of the White House.

Legislators are great at shaking hands, grinning, saying the right thing at the right time, and inventing weasel words to add to the list we provided earlier. You probably wouldn't want your son or daughter to marry one.

Corporate Headhunters

An alternative title is "executive search consultants." Their hobby is collecting people for a fee. A big one.

To a headhunter, any manager is a potential candidate, client, or source. It's often hard to tell which way they want to use you, but it's nice to know several headhunters because they always know the best places for lunch and pick up the check afterward.

Some headhunters have been suspected of being industrial spies. Others are accused of acting for employers who wanted to test an employee's loyalty (or erode it). On balance, even if you assumed their ethics were nonexistent, headhunters couldn't stay in business if they did this often. So it's safe to assume the approaches are valid.

Perhaps the greatest deceit is applied not by headhunters to their targets, but by the targets to their bosses. The comment "I've been contacted by a headhunter" can mean any of the following:

(1) I saw a job advertised, answered the ad, and haven't been rejected yet.

(2) I've been contacted as a source by a headhunter, and I'm too naive to know that he's after the people I know and not me.

(3) I've contacted every headhunter in town, and no one has replied.

(4) Nobody has approached me; I'm just trying to jack up my salary.

Journalists

Journalists don't have much to contribute to management, but you need to watch the press to see what public opinion will do. On business matters, Wall Street tends to form, rather than follow, public opinion. The basic rules for dealing with journalists include

(1) Nominate one person in your organization to deal with queries from the press. If things are going well, that person could be you. If not, delegate the job to somebody else.

(2) Present the constructive side of things. Don't be lured into revealing the negative side unless you can offer specific and credible contradictions.

(3) Don't be deceptive. Experienced journalists have a built-in B.S. detector, and they'll be after you like a school of piranhas. Take the advice of Mark Twain: "When in doubt, tell the truth."

(4) If you can't comment, tell journalists off the record why you can't and when you will. Then meet that deadline.

(5) Brief relevant journalists about the company in advance whenever possible. This ensures that they have accurate information to draw from when a story breaks.

MBAs

Harvard MBAs are perhaps the most notorious, although Yale, Princeton, Dartmouth, and the University of Chicago deserve honorable mention. MBAs in general are multiplying like rabbits, according to

Fortune magazine. The number of MBA grads rose from 43,000 in 1976 to 67,000 just a decade later.

Older students with an MBA deserve a little respect. Most of them have made sacrifices to earn it. Furthermore, they've accumulated enough real-world experience to know that theory doesn't always work in practice.

Newly minted MBAs with no perspective beyond the classroom are another matter. They have the arrogance of youth combined with the self-delusion that their degree is a sure ticket to success. (After all, it was enough to get them a high five-figure starting salary, wasn't it?) As prominent personnel expert Robert Half wryly observed, "An MBA's first shock could be the realization that companies require experience before they hire a chief executive officer."

Youthful MBAs may rely too heavily on their academic background. They haven't realized yet that people make a company run. Until they discover this fact, they may be in for some unpleasant reality checks. Don't let them come of age in your department. Try to shuffle them off on competitors first so they can make their mistakes there. After four or five years of experience, they may be ripe enough to recruit for your outfit.

Companies tend to hire MBAs for their skills and techniques instead of their potential as general managers, and perhaps that's a good idea. Graduation from a business school doesn't always guarantee the personal qualities and management excellence needed to run a profit center or a corporate subsidiary.

If you're reasonably successful at work, there's no guarantee that earning an MBA will do you much good.

Some people go back to school only because they're temporarily unemployed, and conditions may not improve by the time they get out. If you find yourself in that situation, it helps to have social contacts with a few headhunters.

MANAGEMENT LITERATURE

Far too much is written far too seriously about management. Even the most dedicated academic couldn't plow through it all in a lifetime. The glut of business-oriented books now on the market would fill a small-town library.

It's perfectly acceptable for bluffers to ignore most of the trendy business books on the market. In fact, observers noted that several of the so-called "excellent" companies mentioned in Tom Peters and Robert Waterman's *In Search of Excellence* took a nosedive just a year after the book was published. So much for excellence.

Be selective in your management reading, and rejoice in the fact that books are biodegradable or can be donated to the local library. You don't have to be on intimate terms with the latest theory; you only have to know its name. Then, if the new concept proves to have some value after all, you can move on to phase two, in which you keep an open mind while observing that "the idea sounds good, but it hasn't been validated yet."

If the idea continues to grow in popularity, you still don't have to jump on the bandwagon. Move cautiously, insisting on large-scale practical examples of its value over a realistic period. "Realistic," by the way, should be defined in years – not weeks or months.

Few newly invented management theories ever

prove practical enough for real managers to use in practice. You can write most of them off after a discreet waiting period, feeling confident that your reputation has been enhanced by proceeding cautiously instead of being sucked in by a fad.

Several names are safe to use in connection with management theory. Three (Douglas McGregor, Frederick Herzberg, and Abraham Maslow) have already been mentioned. Add to those Peter Drucker, C. Northcote Parkinson, William Ouchi, Dr. Laurence Peter, and Robert Townsend. Some of these, along with several others, are profiled below.

Drucker

Peter Drucker has been around so long that his name is almost synonymous with management itself. Some people swear that he invented the concept. Fortunately, Drucker has written so much that you don't have to remember any one chunk of it. Just absorb it all and forget the source. This is easy because Drucker lives in the real world and doesn't need to hang catchy labels on pet theories in order to be remembered.

Blake and Mouton

Drs. Robert Blake and Jane Mouton are the proud parents of the Managerial Grid that we mentioned earlier. It helps to remember that a 9,9 position on their grid is ideal (concern for people and production is maximized) 1,1 is horrible (concern for people and production is nil) and 5,5 is so-so (you're balancing but not maximizing either one).

Professor C. Northcote Parkinson

This management luminary has produced a large body of light and easily understood work, but he's most famous for Parkinson's First Law, which states, "Work expands so as to fill the time available for its completion." If you want to pose as a scholar of Parkinson, you can also quote his Second Law: "Expenditure rises to meet income. Individual expenditure not only rises to meet income but tends to surpass it."

Bluffers are most likely to encounter Parkinson's First Law when delegating work to subordinates. If you give them a generous deadline to complete a job, they'll typically use all the time available. To make Parkinson's First Law work for you, always compress the schedule a bit. Employees will usually manage to turn in a respectable job by your original deadline. If things get fouled up, however, it's nice to know that you've got a built-in cushion to fall back on.

MANAGEMENT GURUS

Management gurus come and go. Those who stay tend to do so on the strength of their entertainment value instead of their contribution to management. There are a few distinguished exceptions, but their wealth usually comes from their media exposure, not from the fact that they have managed successful businesses.

Gurus are worthwhile in spite of this, because they popularize good management practice. By doing so, they make bad management techniques easier to identify and attack.

Herzberg and Maslow

Frederick Herzberg and Abraham Maslow are both heavy-hitters in the field of motivation. In a bluffer's nutshell, Herzberg said that jobs should contain two sets of factors. The first, maintenance factors, are things that people believe they should get no matter what. These include decent pay, working conditions, and fringe benefits. Maintenance factors don't motivate anybody, but if they're taken away, workers will get mad and quit. So provide them, along with Herzberg's second set of factors, motivational factors. These are a chance to grow within the job and move up the organizational ladder. Praise and a basic liking for the work itself are motivational factors too. So much for Herzberg.

Maslow is famous for his Hierarchy of Needs. This contends that people try to satisfy a sequence of needs starting with physiological needs and progressing through safety, social, ego-esteem, and self-fulfillment. The job can't cover them all, but it can usually cover the bottom two reasonably well. The more management tries to change the work and the organization to satisfy the top three, the happier folks will be. End of Maslow.

Dr. Laurence J. Peter

Dr. Laurence J. Peter did most of his work with emotionally disturbed children. It's no wonder that his main claim to fame is in management theory, because what works in one field almost always applies to the other. Think about it.

All bluffers should memorize the Peter Principle, which states

> In a hierarchy, every employee tends to rise to his level of incompetence.

Peter's corollary is

> In time, every job tends to be occupied by an employee who is incompetent to carry out its duties.

So who's doing the work? Employees who haven't yet reached their level of incompetence.

The Peter Principle, as a book, may be a good example of a parallel principle – that written work tends to be expanded to the point where it loses its impact and thus some, or all, of its merit. For example, a brilliant or pithy concept may be summarized in an article, which receives rave reviews. The author, unfortunately, cannot leave well enough alone. He or she feels compelled to drag the idea out like a string of taffy and ends up with a book that repeats the same message in 40,000 words or more. You'll see this too much in management literature. Good ideas ought to be condensed into slogans that will fit on business cards or bumper stickers. They make more sense that way, and they're easier to remember. And speaking of remembering things, jot down this quote from Dr. Peter. It might be called the Bluffer's Credo: "Competence, like truth, beauty, and contact lenses, is in the eye of the beholder."

John T. Molloy

Malcolm Forbes said, "Looking the part helps get the chance to fill it." John Molloy told people *how* to look the part, and it has probably made him a multimillionaire.

He started in the early 1970s with *Dress for Success*, which was followed by *The Woman's Dress for Success Book*, *John T. Molloy's New Dress for Success*, *How to Work the Competition into the Ground and Have Fun Doing It*, and *Molloy's Live for Success*. He also pioneered a new field of expertise that some people take seriously: wardrobe consultant.

Bluffers need to have at least a nodding acquaintance with Molloy's sartorial advice because we all know that people jump to conclusions. If your clothes imply confidence, power, and authority, then many coworkers will assume that you really *are* confident, powerful, and authoritative. Fake it till you make it.

Managers, like fast-food employees, supermarket cashiers, and garage mechanics, wear uniforms. Theirs may not include nametags, cutesy-poo hats, or rainbow piping on the seams, but the idea is the same. Every organization has a dress code. Supervisors may wear ties, middle managers ties and jackets, and top bosses vested suits. Even in bed. Or so it seems.

Bluffers should realize that there's nothing to keep you from dressing *above* your level. Except, perhaps, your budget. If you look like part of the power structure, others may assume that you are. This gives you a psychological edge over unkempt or out-of-style colleagues, and you also impress those in seats of power (reread Forbes' quote again). Managers are exempt from the truth in packaging law. If you look sharp, people will assume you are. It's as simple as that.

Alfred P. Sloan

Alfred P. Sloan's excellent book *My Years with General Motors* is worth reading. He's considered the father of modern business organization. Another reason for mentioning him here is that he's virtually the only management writer who actually managed a company and did it well. His book followed his experience. Current-day managers who feel the urge to write their memoirs with one foot in the executive suite ought to follow Sloan's example. It also wouldn't hurt to live by one of the many memorable quotes he left behind, including

The primary object of the corporation . . . was to make money, not just motor cars.

No fixed, inflexible rule can ever be substituted for the exercise of sound business judgment in the decision-making process.

J. K. Galbraith

Few economists write well about management. Fewer still can write *and* manage. Indeed, there's a respectable body of support for the theory that being an economist actually *dis*qualifies you from managing anything.

John Kenneth Galbraith is an exception. He has done a lot to make economics understandable to the layman, and even to business managers.

Maybe the best reason why Galbraith sounds more sensible than most economists (aside from the fact that he writes words, not jargon) is his underlying belief that the nature of capitalism has changed during this century, so traditional economic theories no longer apply. This, of course, makes him popular with everyone who hates economists and theories. Galbraith is nobody's fool.

It's not enough to know his name. You should read him too. The book to read, because it's full of warnings about margins, calls, and corporate collapse, is *The Great Crash.* Galbraith thoughtfully points out, in the latest edition, that his book can probably be found at many bookstores, but not on the racks at airport newsstands.

Shepherd Mead

Mead's book *How to Succeed in Business Without Really Trying* produced lots of worthwhile insights on American management. It was later turned into a funny musical starring Robert Morse. The book is extremely practical. For example, he allows managers to have hobbies if they coincide with those of the company president. Bluffers who can't find a copy of *How to Succeed in Business* should watch a video of the movie *The Secret of My Success* starring Michael J. Fox. It's a fair reflection of some of Mead's observations and also one from George Bernard Shaw: "My way of joking is to tell the truth. It's the funniest joke in the world."

JARGON

Jargon is the major obstacle to understanding most business activities – especially those involving management. It may not be correct to say that managers deliberately cover their tracks with a verbal smoke-screen, but the results often suggest that they do.

The use and growth of jargon was originally intended to achieve the opposite result – to make communication clear and precise in areas where traditional words and phrases didn't work very well. The original purpose can't excuse or justify the current situation, however.

Bluffers don't have to reveal their ignorance in order to combat jargon. Simply ask the writer or speaker to simplify the message so it can be understood by the board of directors or rank-and-file employees. This is a handy, all-purpose request which, according to the circumstances, may be modified to include the chairman of the board, management trainees, visitors from other organizations, or accountants. Here are several key examples of jargon.

Behavioral

"Behavioral what?" you might ask. "Behavioral anything" is the answer. Whatever this word precedes is likely to be a complex phrase for something that is quite simple under a more primitive name. Then again, maybe the concept didn't exist a decade or so ago. The word "behavioral" is often used to imply a nebulous network of misunderstood conditions that the speaker or writer blames for whatever has happened that wasn't supposed to happen. This can include anything from low employee morale to disappointing sales figures, fluctuating interest rates, and uncertain foreign political conditions.

Bottom Line

This is the ultimate result. The term comes from accounting, where it refers to the profit or loss that's left after adjustments, good news, bad news, and creative accounting are applied. When in doubt, bluffers should ask, "What's the bottom line?" which really means, in blunt terms, "Give me the worst news and cut the crap."

Impact

This innocent noun has infected business communication like a plague. Self-important mangers may ask, "How will this impact . . . ?" or, worse yet, "This impacted our position . . ." Somehow, managers believe they sound more forceful, aggressive, or authoritative when they use "impact" as a verb. Actually, they just sound pompous and dumb. Wisdom teeth and bowels may *become* impacted under the wrong circumstances, but only inept managers and maladroit bluffers use "impact" as a verb. When you hear it used that way, be on the alert. The user's probably trying to impress somebody. Don't let it be you.

Capitalist

Ignore the dictionary definition of the word "capitalist" because it's often used by detractors as an epithet. Enemies of free enterprise use "capitalist" as a synonym for greedy, money-grubbing, unconscionable managers or companies who will sacrifice Mom and apple pie for the sake of profit. If you have to label yourself or your company, try one of the more positive ones, such as "major employer," "industrialist, "wealth-creator," or perhaps the all-time favorite, "entrepreneur." The last term implies taking great risks for the sake of rewards, and its swashbuckling, Rambo-like connotation grabs people's imaginations. You come across as an economic white knight who is battling tooth and nail to make a few honest bucks in a hard, cruel world. Go for it. "Entrepreneur" sounds more romantic than "capitalist" any day.

CPA

No, this CPA isn't a certified public accountant. It stands for Critical Path Analysis, the process of deciding which steps in a process, project, or task are vital to its completion. Cooks use CPA instinctively when preparing a seven-course dinner. Managers have to learn it.

The question bluffers should ask when something is delayed is, "Is this item on the critical path?" If it isn't, you have some breathing space. If it is, assign somebody to bird-dog the problem until it's resolved and the job is back on schedule again.

Contribution

This is a good word to use on accountants who are trying to get you to accept profit figures that are adjusted for overhead costs — including those that were incorrectly allocated from other managers' projects to yours. It's the corporate version of the old shell game. Now you see it, now you don't.

"Contribution" is gross profit after subtracting variable costs and expenses but *before* subtracting overhead. If your favorite project is about to lose support in favor of another, and they're both being presented on a full-adjusted basis, stand up, pound the conference table, and holler, "We have to look at the relative contributions!" If your project looks bad by this comparison, tough luck. But if your project is making a larger contribution before overhead than the rival one, you can battle to have overhead reevaluated, ignored, or allocated over several projects—especially those of colleagues.

Dedication

Once upon a time, people were dedicated. Some of them still are. Today, however, the word applies more to machines than to people.

Whenever you hear that a machine is "dedicated," that means that it does only one thing. That also means it's doomed to obsolescence by another machine, probably coming off the production line right now, that will do everything the "dedicated" model does and a few dozen other things besides. In the early 1980s, for example, companies bought "dedicated" word processors, which were basically myopic personal computers with a one-track mind. The introduction of multipurpose PCs and a host of business-oriented software from spreadsheets to data bases made dedicated word processors virtually obsolete.

Downstream

This term was coined by the oil industry, but it has since spread to every facet of business. Today, "downstream" is often used to mean the end of a vertically integrated operation nearest to consumers. "Upstream," by contrast, means back at the oil well — or the source.

Onstream

This term is applied to plants, machines, or other facilities that are just about ready to go. A plant comes "onstream" when the doors open. A machine comes "onstream" when somebody throws the switch and it begins to crank out widgets.

Ethics

An obsolete term once used in business. You'll sometimes hear it as a warning signal. Anyone who professes high or indeed *any* standards of business ethics should be mistrusted. To quote Malcolm Forbes once again, "Most people are what they say they're not."

People who are really ethical don't have to advertise the fact, and those who do may only hide behind ethics because it serves their purpose at the time.

People who say "Trust me" or "I guarantee it" fall into this category. Get their words on tape or in writing and have one or two witnesses handy if you can.

Software

This word refers to computer programs. You'll often hear people blame software for problems that they haven't been able to figure out yet. Such folks may say (often with a shrug), "It's a software problem" or "There's a software bug that the vendor's people are trying to straighten out." Bluffers should realize that so-called software problems are often not problems at all. The problem may be that people don't understand how to run the software or how to set up the hardware (computer, printer, and other equipment) correctly.

Interface

This act sounds like it might be illegal, even between consenting adults. It refers to connections between the different pieces of hardware in a computer system. Sometimes interface problems are caused by loose connections or somebody who forgot to plug the darn thing in. So much for high tech.

You may also hear "interface" used as a synonym for two people or departments who decide to communicate with each other. Managers who use "interface" for "meet" or "talk" are likely to use "impact" as a verb. May their numbers decrease.

Fiscal

The word "fiscal" means money. For example, a "fiscal year" is the 12-month period a company uses for accounting purposes. "Fiscal responsibility" means being careful with your money.

People who use the word "fiscal" sound stuffy and artificial. If you *must* use it, pronounce it correctly—*fis-cal*, not *phys-i-cal*. Managers who talk about "physical years" sound like ignoramuses or, worse yet, unemployed high school football coaches.

Leader

As in "market leader." Market leadership can be good or bad. If it results from innovation, it's generally considered to be good, and you should charge high prices while you have the chance. Later, market leaders may be accused of being monopolies, a connotation that's not so good for public image.

Being a leader in a market where anyone can copy and undercut you is a bad thing unless you're prepared to be ruthless about the competition. (Read *Think*, the unapproved story of IBM, for details.) You can also compete with yourself in more than one area, such as some cereal and confectionery companies do.

There are certain markets where it's feasible to be a leader in profit without leading in sales. This makes you a less-visible target; you're not as likely to provoke attacks from competitors and price wars this way.

Logistics

This is another word where the dictionary definition hasn't caught up with current business usage. The dictionary says logistics is the "art of moving, lodging, and supplying troops and equipment," but businesses use it to include all aspects of marketing distribution, including customer awareness. The word is more often applied to "downstream" operations.

Management Information

This generic description applies to any data prepared by nonmanagers such as accountants, analysts, actuaries, market researchers, and the like. Without the label "management information," it wouldn't be recognized as intended for management. Real managers don't call their information anything in particular.

Mix

This is a handy term. There's the marketing mix (product, place, price, and promotion), the product mix (the array of stuff we're selling right now), the financing mix (the stocks and bonds we've sold to raise money), and various other mixes that managers may concoct to get a job done.

When problems arise, the bluffer can usually blame them on difficulty with a mix of some sort. Use your imagination.

PERT

This stands for Program Evaluation and Review Technique, which means much the same as the CPA (Critical Path Analysis) mentioned earlier. Identifying and analyzing the critical path is part of PERT.

Proactive

This is the opposite of reactive, and it's a good thing for bluffers to be. Reactive managers are considered short-sighted and emotional. Bluffers may have to be reactive, however, until they find out what the heck's going on. After they find out, they become proactive. Your progress toward becoming a proactive manager (as well as an assertive one) begins when you first realize what you're *not* being told in a report, memo, or meeting.

Project

"Project" can mean many things, several of them ominous.

For example, there are "capital projects," such as spending huge amounts of money on a new plant or assembly-line robots. There are also "systems projects," which spend huge amounts of money on new computers or custom-designed software. Indeed, the word "project" can be connected with just about any expense of more than five bucks that management wants to sound important and newsworthy.

Perhaps the most suspect projects of all are "special projects." These are typically nonjobs that are created for excess personnel who are either relatives of top managers or washed-up executives who are too dangerous to be laid off or fired. The Manager of Special Projects, of course, supervises the work of all these people, and he or she commands a handsome salary. Nice work if you can get it. The Manager of Special Projects may be the most accomplished bluffer in the company. He probably knows where lots of bodies are buried.

Redundancy

This euphemism for excess personnel became respectable in the early 1980s. Employees who are no longer needed or whose jobs are about to be abolished are declared "redundant." Soon they'll become something else: "unemployed." Of course, these people are never laid off or fired. They're "dehired." Doesn't that sound pleasant?

User Friendly

A term coined by computer people to describe any machine and/or program that's easier for people to use than it was last year. Most equipment and programs started out being user hostile. The more we users complain, the more friendly they get. We should have started complaining sooner.

Challenge

Use this term when you tell your boss about an insurmountable problem. It makes you sound like an eager, confident world-beater. Bosses love workers who view obstacles as challenges. They don't want crybabies who complain about problems. If people bring a "challenge" to you, however, be on your toes. Don't let them toss it in a corner of your office and beat a hasty retreat. You've got enough of your own "challenges" to worry about. Take inventory at the end of the day to be sure the challenges in your custody are yours alone. Kick the rest out.